ROBERT PATTINSON

~ FATED FOR FAME ~

SIMON PULSE

An imprint of Simon & Schuster Children's Publishing Division

1230 Avenue of the Americas, New York, NY 10020

Text copyright © 2008 by Vic Parker

Originally published in Great Britain in 2008 by Piccadilly Press Ltd.

Photo credits:

Getty: p2, p3, p7, p8, p9, p10, p13, p15, p17, p18, p19, p21, p28 (left), p29 (right), p36, p38, p41, p43, p45, p48

Rex Features: p5, p11, p16, p20 (right), p24, p25, p27 (top), p28 (right), p29 (left), p 31 (both) p33, p37

Corbis: p22/23, p26, p27 (bottom), p34/35, p39

Alamy: p20 (left), p46, p47

Designed by Simon Davis

Manufactured in the United States of America

First Simon Pulse paperback edition January 2009

2 4 6 8 10 9 7 5 3 1

Library of Congress Control Number 2008942805

ISBN-13: 978-1-4169-8997-4

ISBN-10: 1-4169-8997-8

ROBERT PATTINSON

~ FATED FOR FAME ~

AN UNAUTHORIZED BIOGRAPHY BY MEL WILLIAMS

Simon Pulse · New York London Toronto Sydney

Meet
Robert Pattinson

Step aside, Orlando Bloom, Daniel Radcliffe, and Jude Law—the next big British movie star is on his way, and his name is Robert Pattinson! And it's official, too—Robert was named British Star of Tomorrow by *Screen International* magazine, which said he "so oozes charm and likeability that casting directors are predicting a big future."

For someone who only started taking a serious interest in acting when he was 15, Robert—or RPattz, as some of his friends call him—has had a truly meteoric rise to fame. However, from his screen-stealing performance as Cedric Diggory in *Harry Potter and the Goblet of Fire* to his heart-stopping portrayal of Edward Cullen in *Twilight*, it's easy to see why. Robert has the rare acting talent and smoldering physical presence all would-be movie stars crave but few are actually lucky enough to possess. Not surprisingly, with his good looks and natural charisma, in the past Robert has also been in demand as a model, under the name Robert Thomas-Pattinson. But did you realize that Robert is even more talented? It's been a well-kept secret up until now, but Robert's also making a name for himself as a musician, under the pseudonym Bobby Dupea.

You might assume that gorgeous, mega-talented Robert is big-headed and aloof.

ROBERT PATTINSON

But if you were lucky enough to get to talk to him, you'd find out the opposite is true—he's friendly and unassuming, and quick to play down his success, putting his soaring career path down purely to chance (as if!).

Want to find out more about the gorgeous guy behind the floppy hair and the chiseled jaw? For instance, what was Robert like at school? What was his very first acting break? What sort of girls does he like? What hopes and dreams does he have for the future? For the answers to these and many other essential questions, just read on. This book will tell you what Robert Pattinson is really like, inside and out.

ROBERT fact file...

Real name: Robert Thomas Pattinson

Stage name: Robert Pattinson

Model name: Robert Thomas-Pattinson

Musician name: Bobby Dupea

Nicknames: Rob, RPattz, Spunk Ransom

Birthday: May 13, 1986

Birthplace: London, England

Height: 6 feet 1 inch

Eyes: Blue-gray (and dreamy!)

Hair: Brownish-blond (and strokeable!)

Parents: Clare and Richard Pattinson

Siblings: Robert has two older sisters, Elizabeth and Victoria

Home: London, England

ome sweet home

ⵐert was born under the star sign of Taurus, so you would expect him to be very close
ⵐis family and happy at home—Taureans are said to love stability and security, to dislike
ⵐnge to their living environment, and to be devoted to their parents and siblings.

Robert's parents have been described as "arty." When Robert was young, his mother,
ⵐre, didn't have an ordinary job in an office or shop, but worked for an agency in the
ⵐmorous world of modeling. Robert has joked that his father, Richard, was a used car
ⵐler, but in fact his work
ⵐs much cooler and more
ⵐlish than that—he ran a
ⵐiness importing vintage
ⵐs from America.

Robert was the baby of
family—and the only
ⵐ. His sister Elizabeth
ⵐhree years older and
ⵐsister Victoria is five
ⵐrs his senior. Robert
ⵐn't seem to mind being
ⵐnumbered by older
ⵐmen, however. In fact,
ⵐet his sisters enjoy
ⵐying at dressing him
ⵐas a girl and calling
ⵐ Claudia—until he was
ⵐyears old!

Robert's roots

Robert grew up in a part of London called Barnes, which is like a quaint village, with characterful old houses and buildings, including a popular arts center called The Old Sorting Office, which is a venue for theater performances. Famous rock and pop stars often hang out in Barnes because there is a renowned recording studio on Church Road called Olympic Studios.

Quick • ROBERT • Quiz

Q) When Robert was a child, how much pocket money did his parents give him?

A) Robert earned his own pocket money. He started doing a paper route when he was about 10, earning $20 per week. He says he was obsessed with earning money until he was about 15.

FAST FACT!

According to Chinese astrology, Robert was born in the Year of the Tiger. Tiger people are charming, with magnetic appeal, and are great fun to be around. However, they can sometimes also be sensitive and moody, and can like to spend time on their own. Sound like Robert?

A musical youth

Music was, in fact, Robert's first love. He started playing the piano when he was about three years old—his feet must have been dangling from the piano stool and his nose hovering just above the keys! Little Robert enjoyed learning how to play so much that he wasn't content with just one instrument. When he was only five, he also began to learn the guitar. He soon became good at performing classical guitar pieces.

Robert was so keen on music and showed such promise that if anyone had predicted what he might grow up to become, they would have been highly likely to say "a musician." His parents must have encouraged all of their children to pursue an interest in music, since Robert's sister Lizzy has in fact gone on to become a professional singer-songwriter.

Robert's childhood passion for music has also lasted his whole life.

COULD DO BETTER!

Robert's first school was a private all-boys school called Tower House, in East Sheen, not far from his home. Like most schools, it had a drama club and Robert took part from the age of six. He acted in several productions, playing the King of Hearts in *Spell for a Rhyme*, a play written by one of his teachers, and playing a minor character, Robert, in an adaptation of William Golding's famous novel *Lord of the Flies*. However, he never stood out as being a great actor. Robert just enjoyed taking part in these school productions as many of his friends did.

In fact, Robert didn't really shine at school at all. If anyone had told the teachers there he would one day play the role of ideal student Cedric Diggory, Head Boy at Hogwarts, they would probably have laughed out loud. Caroline Booth, the school secretary of Tower House, has described Robert as being not particularly academic. In a 1998 newsletter, he was also said to be "a runaway winner of last term's Form Three untidy desk award!" Robert was sometimes naughty, too. For instance, he remembers being a lunch monitor and stealing people's fries!

And here's a mystery for you. At the age of 12, Robert left Tower House, but no one knows why. Thousands of his fans worldwide have nearly been driven crazy with wondering and trying to find out. All Robert has said on the matter is: "I was quite bad." So if you ever get the chance to meet him, see if you can persuade him to tell you!

Must try harder

After leaving Tower House, Robert went to another private school, the Harrodian School in Barnes, which was for both boys and girls. You might think that Robert would have tried to turn over a new leaf—however, he still didn't put much effort into his studies. He never skipped school, because he liked his teachers, but he hardly ever bothered to do his homework. As you can imagine, Robert's report cards were always pretty bad. His parents must have been frustrated, as they were paying expensive school fees for Robert to be a student there.

Robert the rapper

Robert may not have shown much interest in schoolwork, but he was still passionate about music. Although he stopped learning classical guitar at about age 12, he kept up his piano-playing all through his teenage years. Like most young people, Robert got really into popular music—rap in particular. He became a big fan of rap superstar Eminem. Jay Kay, the lead singer of funk band Jamiroquai, also became one of Robert's musical heroes.

ROBERT SAYS . . .

Robert liked his English teacher because she encouraged him to think and write instead of just giving a basic answer to a question. Robert has said: "I used to hand in 20 pages of nonsense and she'd still mark it. She was a really amazing teacher."

Spreading his wings

It must have been clear to Clare and Richard Pattinson from seeing Robert's flair for music that, although their teenage son didn't seem to be suited to do well academically, he would excel if he had opportunities to develop the creative side of his personality.

Because Clare Pattinson worked for a modeling agency, she would have known that her son's good looks and personality would be ideal in front of a camera. It was a natural step to get Robert involved in modeling and he did several photographic jobs from age 12

("when I stopped looking like a girl," as Robert says) to age 15.

Robert's parents must also have begun to wonder whether their son would have a talent for acting. When Robert was 13, he watched the film *One Flew Over the Cuckoo's Nest* and was captivated by the lead actor, megastar Jack Nicholson. Robert has since said: "I used to try and be him in virtually everything I did, I don't know why . . . I dressed like him. I tried to do his accent. I did everything like him."

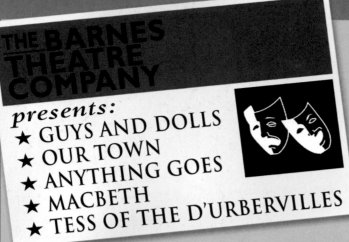

THE BARNES THEATRE COMPANY

presents:
- ★ GUYS AND DOLLS
- ★ OUR TOWN
- ★ ANYTHING GOES
- ★ MACBETH
- ★ TESS OF THE D'URBERVILLES

Into the spotlight

Robert has said, "My dad wanted me to be an actor," and that Richard had some "weird foresight" that acting was what his teenage son should be doing.

One evening when Robert was 15, he was out for dinner with his dad at the Tootsie's hamburger joint in Barnes when they fell into conversation with a group of pretty girls at a nearby table. Richard asked them where they had been, and they replied that they were friends from a local drama group, the Barnes Theatre Company, which was based just around the corner from the Pattinsons' house.

Right afterward, Richard said, "Son, that is where you need to go." He kept nagging Robert about it for so long that Robert eventually gave in and joined. He didn't agree to take part in the acting, but just said he'd be part of the backstage crew—and he was only finally persuaded because he knew he'd be surrounded by attractive would-be actresses like the girls he'd met in Tootsie's.

ROBERT SAYS . . .
Once when Robert was asked by an interviewer what his motivation was for starting acting, he said it was "a social thing. I literally went there one hundred percent to meet these girls sitting at the next table."

Addicted to acting!

The Barnes Theatre Company was run by experienced actors who put on two shows per year, produced to a very high standard. Everyone involved was so enthusiastic that, after working behind the scenes on one play, Robert thought perhaps he'd take his dad's advice after all and give acting a go. The next show was to be the musical *Guys and Dolls*, and, when the auditions came around, Robert put himself forward to be in front of the scenery this time, not behind it. He even wanted to play the lead—the character of Nathan Detroit, who in the movie version of the show was played by the legendary singer and actor Frank Sinatra. So

did Robert win the starring role? No, he was given a very small background part as a Cuban dancer. But Robert wasn't put off. He took on the role and performed it the best he could—even though he found it somewhat embarrassing!

The next show was a three-act play by Thornton Wilder called *Our Town*, which follows the everyday lives of citizens in small-town America in the early twentieth century—particularly the life of doctor's son George Gibbs. And this time Robert *did* win a lead role—the character of George himself. He gave a brilliant performance and from then on there was no holding him back. Robert appeared in several other amateur productions, such as the musical *Anything Goes* (as Lord Evelyn Pakleigh), the Shakespeare play *Macbeth* (as Malcolm, the King of Scotland), and a play adaptation of Thomas Hardy's classic novel *Tess of the D'Urbervilles*—in which he played a lead role, the villainous character of Alec Stoke-d'Urberville. Robert's acting was so outstanding that a theatrical agent who was on the lookout for new talent approached him and signed him up!

№ 2093

ADMISSION

Robert's career takes off

It wasn't long before Robert's agent had found him auditions for several professional acting jobs. First, Robert won the supporting role of Giselher in a film to be made for TV called *The Ring of the Nibelungs*. You can imagine how thrilled 17-year-old Robert was about the opportunity—not only because he would appear on-screen rather than onstage, but also because the movie was going to be shot in South Africa, plus he was going to get paid for acting for the very first time! However, as it turned out, he didn't spend his money on anything luxurious. . . .

When Robert excitedly told his parents he had landed the part, his dad suggested that he should leave school, since, on top of not working very hard, he was now going to be taking four months off schoolwork for filming. However, Robert was insistent that he wanted to stay on and take his exams. So his dad said that Robert could use his earnings to pay his own school fees, and he would pay him back if his exam results were good enough!

A life-changing audition

2003

The year 2003 proved to be extremely big for Robert.

The day before Robert had to fly out to film *The Ring of the Nibelungs*, he went to a meeting that had been arranged for him with Mike Newell, who was to be the director of the fourth Harry Potter movie, *Harry Potter and the Goblet of Fire*. Robert tried out for the part of Cedric Diggory. Can you believe he didn't know much about the Harry Potter books and hadn't seen any of the previous movies? He skim-read *Harry Potter and the Goblet of Fire* just the day before the audition. But Robert went into the meeting in a brilliant mood because he was so looking forward to traveling to South Africa to start filming. Robert has said about the audition for the part of Cedric: "I went in with this complete confidence—I was convinced I had it."

As is usual with auditions, Robert didn't hear then and there if he had gotten the part. He put the meeting with Mike Newell to the back of his mind and threw himself into the experience of his first film acting job. But, on the very day he arrived back in London, he had to go for a call-back audition—and was told he had won the part of Cedric Diggory!

MOVIE·STAR GLAMOUR?

After the blockbuster success of the first three Harry Potter movies, not to mention the phenomenon of the series of books themselves, both Robert and his agent knew that appearing as Cedric would bring the young actor to the attention of an enormous worldwide audience. However, Robert didn't have time to think about how his life might soon change.

He had just two weeks before he had to take his exams . . . and his results were an A and two Bs! Robert has said: "I don't know how that happened. I didn't even know half the syllabus. I'd lost faith in the exam system at that point."

Next Robert went straight on to shoot a small part in the film version of the classic novel *Vanity Fair*, starring one of Hollywood's leading actresses, Reese Witherspoon. However, he learned the hard way that just because you take part in filming, it doesn't mean for sure that you will see yourself on the big screen. For the main cinema version of *Vanity Fair*, all of Robert's scenes ended up on the cutting-room floor! You can still see him a few times in the DVD version of the movie, though, if you pay close attention.

Luckily, this wasn't to happen with the role of Cedric Diggory!

Quick · ROBERT · Quiz

Q) What role did Robert play in the movie *Vanity Fair*?

A) The older version of character Rawdy Crawley, son of the lead character, Becky Sharp.

Hello, Hogwarts

The filming of *Harry Potter and the Goblet of Fire* was movie-making on a scale Robert could never have dreamed of. In fact, few actors ever get the chance to be involved in such a humongous blockbuster in their entire career. Here's why:

The book—the fourth in the series—had been subject to even more hype than the others, because one of the main characters actually dies in the story. (The character was of course Cedric Diggory, to be played by Robert.) The filming of the movie was going to take an entire year. The sets were enormous and elaborate—including a 34-foot-deep pool and a maze with hydraulically-operated hedges. Shooting many of the scenes required around 2,000 people on set!

The film was to feature some of the most distinguished names in the British acting industry, such as Oscar-nominated Ralph Fiennes and Maggie Smith, Alan Rickman (the Sheriff of Nottingham in Kevin Costner's *Robin Hood: Prince of Thieves*), Gary Oldman (whom you may know from the Batman movies), David Tennant (TV's *Doctor Who*), Robbie Coltrane (Mr. Hyde in *Van Helsing*), and Miranda Richardson (whom you may have seen in *Fred Claus*).

It's no wonder that to begin with, Robert felt daunted and apprehensive—like many of the young actors involved. To help the Hogwarts students relax and bond with each other, a week was arranged before filming began when they did lots of improvisation as way of getting to know each other and getting into their characters. Robert often paired up with Rupert Grint, who plays the character of Ron Weasley.

Fortunately for Robert, when shooting began, the first scene he had to film—the challenge in the maze—involved only Daniel Radcliffe (Harry Potter), the producer, and a crew of about 150 people. It was good to have this less overwhelming start to filming before he was plunged into the maelstrom of activity on the massive sets of later scenes. Then, inexperienced Robert tried to be supersmooth as a way of coping with his nerves. He has said: "I was a real prat for the first month. I didn't talk to anyone. I just drank coffee and told everyone I was 24 and this famous theater actor just back from South Africa." But soon 18-year-old Robert settled into the experience and relaxed back into being his usual likable self.

What did Robert think about his young co-stars in *Harry Potter and the Goblet of Fire?*

Robert has said that it's weird being around the three main stars of the Harry Potter films, because they're so famous that they're well on their way to becoming icons! But as he worked with them closely for nearly a year, he made and stayed really good friends with his co-stars.

Daniel Radcliffe (Harry Potter): Daniel is three years younger than Robert but Robert thought that he was already an acting pro. He has said: "He's so far superior to me in terms of desirability . . . I think Dan could steal anybody's girlfriend!"

Rupert Grint (Ron Weasley): Robert is two years older than Rupert, with whom he got along particularly well. Robert has said: "He's incredibly funny as a real person." Robert thinks that Rupert is a really versatile actor.

Emma Watson (Hermione Granger): Emma first said she wanted to be an actress at the age of six, but she had only acted in school plays before the Harry Potter movies. Robert has said: "She's an incredibly intelligent young person."

Stanislav Ivanevski (Viktor Krum):
Bulgarian-born Stanislav was spotted by a
Harry Potter casting director while attending
an international school in London. Robert
has said: "I started on the same day as
Stan. Stan and I did a lot of on-screen stuff
together, so we bonded well."

Katie Leung (Cho Chang): Katie waited in line for four hours to get her two-minute audition
for the part of Cho. Robert has said: "I get on really well with Katie, she's a really cool girl."

Clémence Poésy (Fleur Delacour): Clémence's father is an actor, theater director,
and playwright who gave her her first professional acting job when she was 14. She had a
number of film, TV, and stage roles before *Goblet of Fire.* Robert and Clémence have stayed
good friends even though she lives in France and he's
based in England.

Shaping up

An interviewer once inquired what similarities Robert thought he shared with his character, Cedric. He replied: "I am generally quite pleasant—I think he is too . . . I've got blond hair . . . and I am relatively sporty." However, at the start of filming, people didn't think Robert was sporty enough! Cedric is meant to be the sports star at Hogwarts and so, of course, Robert had to look superfit—he even had to appear in a pair of swimming trunks! Robert can remember, when he was trying on the swimming trunks, the costume designer said, "Aren't you supposed to be fit? You could be playing a sissy poet or something!" Right away, he was given a personal trainer—one of the Harry Potter stunt team, all of whom Robert has described as "the most absurdly fit guys in the world." The stunt man drew up a rigorous program of workouts, which Robert found extremely difficult—at the time, he couldn't even do ten pushups!

On top of his punishing exercise schedule, Robert and the other Triwizard Tournament entrants had to have diving training. He remembers: "We had to do this scene looking like heroes diving into the lake. They had a stand-in doing perfect dives on the first take. Then Stan, Clémence, and I tried, but none of us could dive in right, and we all looked really stupid." Robert had to do scuba lessons for the underwater filming too. He learned in a small practice tank and found it fairly easy. But he has said: "I didn't see the big tank until they first started shooting in it. It was about a hundred times bigger than the practice tank and it was so much deeper, so that was sort of scary . . ."

In fact, most of Robert's scenes were action scenes, whether it was fighting off the attacking branches in the maze, battling a dragon, or clashing with evil wizards. The eleven months of filming were draining, yet exhilarating.

Life after Cedric

When Robert finished filming *Goblet of Fire*, he was exhausted. As with all films on this scale, there would be months of post-production work before the movie was released and Robert would become known across the world as the Hogwarts hero, Cedric. In the meantime, Robert said his instinct was "just to sort of collapse." The next sort of work he wanted was definitely a short project—either a very small-scale film or perhaps a short run in a theater play, for a complete change. In May 2005, Robert landed a part in a West End play at the Royal Court Theatre called *The Woman Before*. However, rehearsals did not go well—maybe he was just too worn out after the acting marathon that was *Goblet of Fire*? He was fired shortly before opening night! Reflecting on the experience, Robert once explained: "The acting's come along by accident. I've never trained or anything . . . On *Harry Potter* I was so conscious of the fact that I didn't know what I was doing, I used to sit on the side of the set throwing up. I think I will go to drama school . . . I need to learn some of the fundamentals—like how to act!"

Quick•ROBERT•Quiz

Q) What was Robert's worst experience during the filming of *Goblet of Fire*?

A) He found it extremely embarrassing to dance to rock band in the Yule Ball scene. He enjoyed learn the choreographed dancing, like the waltz, but ther wasn't any training for the rock band dancing—the actors had to be themselves and just go for it!

An overnight sensation

Of course, hanging over Robert was the knowledge that the three previous Harry Potter films had been massive blockbuster successes and the whole world was eagerly waiting for *Goblet of Fire* as the next installment. Robert was immensely nervous about what the fans and critics would think of his performance. For months before the world premiere in November he had nightmares about the star-studded event—huge showbiz names like Madonna had been invited to watch! Robert has said he was so jittery, he couldn't decide what to wear. So he went to Jasper Conran and picked out "the most ridiculous, extravagant clothes—they looked really good in the shop. And then I put them on and I thought: 'You look such an idiot!'"

On the night of Sunday, November 6, 2005, Robert walked up the red carpet to the Leicester Square Odeon in front of around 12,000 clamoring Harry Potter fans and a barrage of the world's press. Many of the media

and fans had camped out all night in the winter cold to ensure they got good vantage points! Afterward, Robert said: "I was in a trance the whole way through it. The day before, I was just sitting in Leicester Square, happily being ignored by everyone. Then suddenly strangers are screaming your name. Amazing!"

The opening of *Harry Potter and the Goblet of Fire* turned out to be the most successful movie opening ever in the UK—the film took $29.8 million in its first weekend. That year, it earned over $896 million worldwide, making it the highest-grossing film of 2005. The DVD became the fastest-selling DVD of all time. And while fans worldwide flocked in their millions to see it, the critics applauded the film too—particularly the way the young leads portrayed the emerging maturity of their teenage characters, putting across subtle emotions and dealing with the dark overall tone.

Suddenly, every entertainment show and magazine worldwide wanted interviews and photographs of the *Goblet of Fire* stars—and all at once, everyone seemed to know Robert's name and instantly recognize his face. He could no longer go out without paparazzi tracking him down and members of the public stopping him in the street and asking for his autograph.

Swamped by attention, Robert's was totally transformed. He said at the time: "It is unbelievable that this stroke of luck completely changed my entire life. I can't even remember what I was thinking two years ago." Whichever way would his career take him next?

ROBERT SAYS . . .
"Harry Potter is what made me become an actor. I credit Harry Potter with everything else that's come since for me."

A CAREER CROSSROADS

After his screen-stealing performance as Cedric Diggory in *Harry Potter and the Goblet of Fire*, Robert found himself widely acclaimed in the British press as "the next Jude Law." As someone who had never had any serious drama training, the pressure on him to find outstanding productions in which he could turn out amazing performances must have been immense. Marked out as a hot young talent, Robert signed with an American agent in LA, and found himself being flown out to all sorts of meetings with Hollywood movie producers to discuss upcoming possible projects.

However, Robert wasn't at all sure what it would be best for him to do to develop his acting ability. He was offered some big contracts—but they seemed too overwhelming. For instance, he was once asked to sign up for three films at a time, a huge commitment that the uncertain young actor wasn't comfortable with. And in some cases, the scripts Robert felt were right for him didn't come his way—for instance, in auditions for one part Robert really wanted, he got down to the last two . . . and then the casting people picked the other actor!

FAST FACT!

You can see Robert reprise his role as Cedric Diggory in the fifth Harry Potter movie: *Harry Potter and the Order of the Phoenix*, which opened in 2007. But this is actually a "flashback" scene from *Goblet of Fire*.

ROBERT SAYS . . .

Robert doesn't moan about the long hours and intense effort involved in filming, and he doesn't let the cutthroat aspect of auditions and ruthless side of show business get him down. He has said: "Sometimes I think, 'To hell with acting,' and then I realize I could be working at a shoe shop. Acting is much cooler."

One thing Robert did know for sure was that after Harry Potter he wanted to test himself by doing "something weird," as he once put it. And he was prepared to wait for the right role to come along. As he said at the time: "I don't really know what I should be doing yet, so I prefer to do nothing really!"

A WALK ON THE DARK SIDE

The perfect opportunity Robert was waiting for turned out to be a TV film called *The Haunted Airman*, which appeared on the BBC in 2006. Based on a 1948 novel by Dennis Wheatley called *The Haunting of Toby Jugg*, the film tells the story of a wounded, traumatized World War II RAF pilot (Toby Jugg—played by Robert) who is sent to a mental institution in Wales, under the watchful eyes of his aunt and his psychiatrist. Toby suffers from guilt and paranoia that manifest as terrors and visions—or perhaps he's actually imprisoned in a private hell and tormented by the spirits of the dead . . .

2006

If there was ever a part more different from the beautiful, heroic Cedric Diggory—and one that would really challenge an actor's abilities—this was it. Toby Jugg was a complex, tortured, and slightly deranged character, and Robert gave a brilliant performance, even though he was confined to a wheelchair all the way through. A reviewer in *The Stage* said: "Pattinson—an actor whose jawline is so finely chiseled it could split granite—played the airman of the title with a perfect combination of youthful terror and world-weary cynicism." Surely now Robert began to feel that his acting capabilities were living up to his fame.

The lighter side of Robert

After fighting dragons in *Goblet of Fire* and demons in *The Haunted Airman*, Robert next turned his hand to something much more light-hearted and up-to-date. This was a modern comedy-drama TV series that aired in 2007—an adaptation of a novel by Kate Long called *The Bad Mother's Handbook*. The story followed a year in the lives of three different types of mother: a thirtysomething woman named Karen; her mother, Nan; and her 17-year-old daughter, Charlie, all trying to live together in the same very small house, and all with their own problems and secrets.

2007

Robert played the part of Daniel Gale, a socially awkward young man who develops a crush on Charlie—even though she has just been dumped by her boyfriend and discovered that she's

pregnant. It was huge fun for him to act alongside talented comedienne and actress Catherine Tate (who played Karen)—who had had huge success with her sketch program, *The Catherine Tate Show*. Working with BAFTA-nominated artists such as Catherine Tate, Anne Reid (who played Nan), and director Robin Sheppard taught Robert yet more new, crucial lessons about the skills involved in different types of acting. You could say that instead of having gone to drama school for training, Robert had set out to learn on the job.

PROD. NO. The Bad Mother's Handbook
SCENE 2   TAKE 1   ROLL
SOUND
DATE Nov 2006
PROD. CO.
DIRECTOR
CAMERAMAN

The BIG SCREEN beckons once again

By now, Robert must have felt he was ready in both his personal and professional life to take on another blockbuster Hollywood movie. He won an irresistible role—that of a vampire who is 108 years old yet appears to be only 17, and who has the ability to read minds, along with superhuman speed and strength! This is, of course, the part of Edward Cullen in the movie *Twilight*.

The film is based on the 2005 novel of the same name by Stephenie Meyer—a book that was translated into 20 languages, became a *New York Times* bestseller, and won awards such as *Publishers Weekly*'s Best Book of the Year, Amazon.com Best Book of the Decade So Far, and an American Library Association Top Ten Best Book for Young Adults accolade.

The plot of *Twilight* has been described as a Gothic Romeo-and-Juliet-type love story. Seventeen-year-old Isabella Swan moves to the small town of Forks, Washington, to live with her father. She is captivated by a mysterious classmate, Edward Cullen, and they fall deeply in love—despite the fact that Edward is a vampire. But Bella's life becomes endangered when three nomadic vampires arrive in town. Can Edward and his family save her—and themselves?

Q) Does Robert like watching horror movies?

A) He has said: "I don't like that 'hiding behind doors' element when suddenly it's like, 'Boo!' I like the more eerie and disturbing horror flicks. One of my favorites is The Exorcist."

ROBERT SAYS . . .

"The thing I found interesting [about Edward] is that he is essentially the hero of the story but violently denies he is the hero."

Living up to expectations

The novel was the first in a series and Robert was aware before he even started filming the movie adaptation that the books had an enormous fan base worldwide—which was still growing fast. As a result, the film—released at the end of 2008—drew a huge following from the moment the cast was announced.

Robert must have been horrified to find that postings were instantly appearing all over the Internet from fans of the book who weren't at all happy that he had been cast as their hero, Edward. There was even an online petition to protest! Some readers moaned that Robert didn't have the right looks to portray Edward the way Stephenie Meyer had described him. Other readers complained that having seen Robert die as the wholesome blond Cedric Diggory, they would never be convinced by him as an all-powerful, mysterious vampire. However, as soon as trailers and scene-snippets from the movie were screened, fan opinion did a drastic turnaround. Suddenly "Twilighters" across the globe couldn't get enough of Robert as Edward—there was an online petition with thousands of signatures in support of him playing the role, and instead of hate mail, Robert was e-mailed marriage proposals! The director of the movie, Catherine Hardwicke, has said: "I feel like a genius to have chosen him for the part."

FAST FACT!

Robert's *Twilight* co-star Kristen Stewart (Bella Swan) is four years younger than him. Her father is a TV producer and her mother is a scriptwriter. She has acted since childhood, playing alongside superstars such as Jodie Foster, Sharon Stone, and Dennis Quaid. Robert has said: "Kristen is the best actress of our generation."

Quick • ROBERT • Quiz

Q) Who is Robert's favorite-ever vampire?

A) He likes the original *Nosferatu*, Max Schreck.

Robert gets intimate

Making *Twilight* was a totally different experience for Robert from filming *Harry Potter and the Goblet of Fire*.

For the very first time, Robert had to put on an American accent for the part. Robert even spoke in his American accent between takes, so he didn't run the risk of slipping in and out of it during filming.

Besides the fact that Cedric Diggory is a supporting part and Edward Cullen is a lead role, the personalities of the two characters are very different Also, Robert's scenes as Cedric Diggory were largely action-oriented, whereas being Edward was often intense, up-close, and personal. Robert has said that *Twilight* is "just about a love story rather than a massive adventure and an entire world," like *Goblet of Fire*.

Robert had to get used to doing lots of kissing in front of his co-stars and film crew, as the key relationship scenes required Robert to kiss Kristen Stewart (lucky girl!).

The "Daniel Radcliffe" of *Twilight*?

In July 2008, five months before the movie was due to premiere, Robert and some of his co-stars appeared at a huge convention for superhero, fantasy, and sci-fi fans called Comic-Con in San Diego. Robert was highly nervous, as 6,500 die-hard *Twilight* fans had traveled there to meet the actors in person and participate in a panel discussion and autograph-signing session—the line to get into the *Twilight* area of the convention stretched for three-quarters of a mile around the building!

However, as it turned out, Robert had nothing to worry about. He took the stage to shrieks of "We love you!" and questions like "Boxers, briefs, or nothing?"

Judging by the reaction of the fans at Comic-Con, *Twilight* is set to be a movie phenomenon that will rocket Robert into acting megastardom. When asked what it's like to be the star of such an anticipated film, Robert answered: "It's kind of terrifying in a lot of ways. I still can't come to terms with it."

Fortunately for us, the director of *Twilight*, Catherine Hardwicke, has predicted that there are even greater things to come from Robert. "His career could be extremely unique," she has said. "He's a powerful, sexy leading man and slips incredibly well into different periods and styles. I'd love to see him work on Tim Burton–esque films where he has the opportunity to create completely wild, original characters that become classics."

Watch out, Johnny Depp—
Robert Pattinson's right behind you!

ROBERT AT HOME

MONDAY
Audition

TUESDAY
learn script

WEDNES
Home/Barn

Robert has never wanted to be famous and has certainly never set out to achieve mega-stardom. In a February 2008 interview he said: "I can't see any advantage to it, because I'm happy with the life I have now." He likes to keep his personal life low-key and private.

Robert lives with a friend in a rented apartment in Soho, London, although he often has to

spend time in Hollywood for meetings and wherever else in the world he is filming. When he's in the UK, he likes just hanging out with his family and close friends. Although he has become good pals with many of his acting co-stars, his best friends are the same two friends he has had since he was 12. When he's with them he can just be Robert from Barnes, instead of feeling like Robert the movie star.

Robert isn't a show-off, flashy type of person. He doesn't own a car and he doesn't have a walk-in wardrobe full of designer labels. In fact, he still wears a lot of the same clothes he did when he was 17. Robert has said in the past that his fashion inspiration is the 1950s actor James Dean—who was famous for his relaxed jeans-and-leather-jacket look.

Life in the spotlight

THURSDAY
Meeting up

Robert has rocketed to fame so fast that he is still getting used to the whole idea of being a celebrity. He often feels overwhelmed and slightly mystified about all the attention he gets and how complete strangers greet him like a long-lost friend and seem to know all about him. Robert has said: "I'm always just sort of terrified as soon as one person starts to recognize me. . . . But when people come up they're always really nice anyway."

The fun side of fame is that Robert is often invited to attend glitzy award ceremonies and showbiz parties, like the MTV movie awards. You might think that celebs would never get tired of going to these glamorous star-studded bashes—but in fact these press-filled events can get quite tiresome after a while. The same as you or I, Robert often loves just slipping out for a pizza or to the movies. However, the downside of his success is that he can no longer go out to a bar or restaurant—or even stroll in a park—without people constantly calling out to him, coming up to him for an autograph and photo, and even trying to chat him up. Robert is delighted to have so many fans, and he'll always do his best to stop and talk to everyone—but it just isn't always possible or he'd never get anywhere!

Quick · ROBERT · Quiz

Q) What sort of music does Robert like best?

A) Robert loves all music, everything from James Brown (soul/funk) to Rachmaninoff (classical).

Robert *at* WORK AND PLAY

In the past, Robert has said that acting came about "by accident" and that landing his breakthrough role in *Goblet of Fire* was "a stroke of luck"—however, this doesn't mean that he takes his career flippantly. Robert gives one hundred and ten percent effort to whichever role he is playing, and he is constantly striving to improve his art by learning new acting skills. He gives his all to any other training that's required for his roles too, such as physical training for stunts and dialogue coaching for different accents.

When Robert's filming, his days are long and exhausting. He may be called to a set as early as 5:30 in the morning to get into makeup and costume. In between movies and plays, Robert's life is a whirl of flying back and forth between Britain and Hollywood to talk to movie directors, casting agents, and producers, and to go for auditions. Robert has a no-nonsense approach to the business side of his career. "I like meetings [in LA] a lot. You go in, no one cares if you're a nice person or not. You just do it—and if you can do it, you do it, and if you can't, you can't."

In his time off, Robert enjoys playing sports. He likes a game of soccer now and then and—when he gets the opportunity for a longer break—to go snowboarding. To relax, Robert likes nothing better than to immerse himself in playing the piano or guitar. He also likes chilling out with his friends over a game of pool—and he's addicted to watching *X-Factor* and *American Idol* on TV.

ROBERT'S FAVORITES
- **Childhood cartoon:** *Sharkey and George*
- **Girly movie:** *Pippi Longstocking*
- **Comic-book superhero:** Gambit from the *X-Men*
- **Burger joint:** In-N-Out Burger
- **Website:** YouTube

FAST FACT!
Robert is very much in demand as a model. He was the face of the 2007 autumn/winter advertising campaign for Hackett luxury menswear.

Lucky in love?

Robert's first kiss was at the age of 12—and
with his dreamboat looks he's hardly been short of potential girlfriends since.
Of course, even top models fall at his feet—such as his ex-girlfriend and Elite model
Nina Schubert. And in turn, because Robert's working alongside stunningly beautiful
actresses all the time, it's not surprising that he sometimes falls for his co-stars—
just ask Katie Leung (Cho Chang in *Goblet of Fire*), whom Robert dated from 2005
to 2006.

But, despite being able to go out with almost any beautiful, talented young woman
he wants, Robert doesn't consider himself to be a ladies' man. He once joked, "Looking
for supermodels takes up my time!" when he meant exactly the opposite. He's just as
happy to be without a relationship, concentrating on his career, his family, and his
friends, as he is to be with a girlfriend.

However, if you hope to become the future Mrs. Pattinson, here's
what you need to know . . .
♥ As a Taurus, Robert's most compatible with girls born under Virgo
and Capricorn, while he'd also get along with Cancerians and Pisceans.
If you're a Libra or Sagittarius, opposites may well attract! ♥ Are
you at all like Robert's *Twilight* co-star Kristen Stewart? Robert has described her as
his celebrity crush. ♥ Could you put up with Robert talking all the time?
He says that speaking too much is his worst habit! ♥ Lastly,
leave your UGG boots at home. Robert can't stand them.

To be seen on screen . . .

So what's next for soon-to-be megastar Robert Pattinson? Well, *Twilight* is the first in a series—so the hottest vampire in history will hit the big screen again in the future. Meanwhile, Robert's played the lead in three other movies, soon to be released.

In *The Summer House*, he stars as Richard, a young man who cheats on his girlfriend and goes off with his new love, only to be dumped in turn—whereupon he decides he'll do whatever it takes to win his girlfriend back.

How to Be is a British-made comedy in which Robert plays a very different role—that of an insecure, depressed social misfit named Art. Robert's performance has already gained widespread praise. A reviewer from the online magazine themovie-fanatic.com said: "You'll get to see Robert Pattinson as an emerging actor with such potential you'll simply want to watch more and more of his films." The role of Art has also won Robert his first international film award—that of Best Actor in a Feature Film at the 2008 Strasbourg International Film Festival.

Perhaps Robert's next award will be for his portrayal of artist Salvador Dali in the movie *Little Ashes*, which tells the story of Dali's rumoured homosexual love affair with the Spanish poet Federico Garcia Lorca. Robert has said: "I think people might be surprised—but I didn't want to get stuck in pretty, public-school roles." Robert's decision to take a career risk by choosing to play a character who has a gay relationship has been compared to Heath Ledger's decision to undertake *Brokeback Mountain*—and surely his performance will earn him similar worldwide admiration.

FAST FACT!

Robert is not fazed by playing intimate raunchy scenes—in his audition for *Twilight*, when he had only just met co-star Kristen Stewart (who had already been cast as Bella), he had to act out a love scene on director Catherine Hardwicke's own bed!

ROBERT SAYS . . .

Robert once commented that he has found trying to "play beautiful" one of the most daunting aspects of acting—even more intimidating than meeting Lord Voldemort! He has said: "It kind of puts you off a little bit, when you're trying to act, and you're trying to get good angles to look good-looking!"

Making music

While Robert's acting talents are on the big screen for all to see, he tries to keep his potential as a musician under wraps. He always tries to underplay the fact that he played a few gigs with a rock band called Bad Girls that he formed with some friends. In interviews he also tries to avoid the fact that he writes his own songs—under the pseudonym Bobby Dupea. Robert's voice is raw and his melodies are folksy and bluesy, reminiscent of the legends Bob Dylan, Emmylou Harris, and Van Morrison.

However, the world is soon going to hear Robert's considerable musical talent as two of his songs feature in the movie *Twilight*. Robert has said: "I was doing music before . . . and Catherine Hardwicke [the director] heard it and then put some of my songs in the cut. I was kind of very, like, terrified about it all." Hardwicke herself has commented: "[Pattinson] is a great pianist—long vampire fingers! . . . His two songs are pretty great."

The only way is up . . .

As well as being an acting star and a rising musician, Robert has many other exciting future ambitions. Multitalented Robert has started writing his own film scripts—and one of them, based on diaries he kept as a teenager, is already being considered by an agent. He has also said that in ten years' time he'd like to have his own film production company—and he'd like to try his hand at theater directing too.

One thing's for certain, Robert's got the talent, the looks, and the personality to be a success in whichever path he chooses in the future, whether it's acting, music, screenwriting, or directing—or another pursuit entirely.

Watch out, world, here comes Mr. Pattinson!